CAST DOWN
BUT NOT
DESTROYED

LIFE WITHOUT A LIMB

A Journal of My Journey

BY BISHOP TETO T. SAUNDERS

CAST DOWN BUT NOT DESTROYED

ISBN: 978-0-9719941-9-5

IN DEDICATION

This project was over 25 years in the making. Every word is heartfelt and expresses my inner experiences during this journey. This book is dedicated my father Teto Thomas Williams, my grandmother Vivian Hudgins, and church mother Navella Bassette. They all transitioned during the coronavirus global pandemic that began in 2020. Each of their impacts in life and death served as motivation for me to finish writing "Cast Down but not Destroyed."

TABLE OF CONTENTS

FOREWARD

Bishop Teto T. Saunders has been a gracious giant since the time I met him over ten years ago. He has proven to be not just a ministry colleague, but a friend and brother who has stood by me through some of my most challenging moments and experiences. This is perhaps as a result of his loving and caring heart along with his passion to minister to those in need of healing whether it be spiritual, mental, emotional or even physical. I have known him to be a true caregiver to those sick at home or in the hospital, the bereaved, the lonely, depressed and even the suicidal. His ability to see beyond faults and flaws to focus on the heart of not just the matter, but the actual person is both genuine and authentic.

As someone who has lived nearly half a century and worked with many, both professionally and in ministry I have been blessed with a vast and rich reservoir of experiences. Having written a couple of my own bodies of work, and to have had the pleasure of editing several for other writers, I've come to recognize what is going to likely be an interesting or worthy read. With so much to consider such as trends, interest, demographics and target audience, a lot goes into the process of ensuring that the investment of time and energy to produce pages that are hopefully filled with not just potential but true purpose will be well served. Unfortunately, I've come across my fair share of literary works that did not seem to possess the needed ingredients to have the reader rushing to get to the next page or make it a challenge to let go of the book.

When I first learned of the vision and concept of this book, I knew immediately that Teto T. Saunders was the right person to author this work. To know who he is without knowing his story is to be void of the realization of his tremendous tenacity and strength. This man was born to be not just a survivor, but an overcomer. The details of his life that you will read throughout the upcoming pages are not just truth, but a testimony of God's goodness and love for His creation.

I encourage you to not only read the words in this book, but to hear the voice of its author. Hear his voice as he tells his story. Hear his voice as he shares his experience, the good, the challenge and especially the victory. Hear his voice as he allows you inside what is perhaps the most tragic experience he will ever have to endure. Hear him and be reminded of the amazing God that we serve.

Bishop A. Bernard Hector
Author of *"Kingdomology 101"* and *"ALL is W.E.L.L."*
Presiding Bishop
Kingdom Covenant Network

ACKNOWLEDGMENTS

First acknowledgment is to my Mother Arlene Williams for always supporting everything in my life. Her morning text to remind me that I am loved each day, pushes me dai ly.

There are not enough ways to say thank you to the late Bishop Robert M. Taylor Sr. Pastor of the Fellowship Tabernacle Church in Philadelphia PA. and Statesville NC., for preparing me for the path of Pastoral Ministries. His voice has guided me in many discussions since June of 1990. His public affirmation and private mentorship have molded me into who I am today.

Extreme gratitude to Dr. Doral R. Pulley and Bishop A. Bernard for believing in me and encouraging me to follow my heart and thoughts for *Cast Down but not Destroyed*.

Special thanks to New Birth Fellowship Tabernacle Church and New Birth Fellowship Alliance for filling in the spaces and places as I embarked on this journey.

I have met some amazing people along this life journey. There are some that have expressed themselves in the testimony chapter. I want to personally thank each of you for purpose in my life journey.

To my brothers and sisters, we are *"better together"* I love each of you!

To the nieces and nephews, you are my village.

To all my peoples from elementary school to present day.... I love each of you!

To *"My Guy"* Alfonso Richardson thank you from the depths of my heart bro. for pushing me, listening to me, and encouraging me at my moment of awakening.

#CCC4Life

Thank you, Brittney Robinson, Yolanda Jenkins and Adriann Bautista for helping me transcribe my thoughts into written text. I would not have been able to do this without each of you.

INTRODUCTION

Cast Down but Not Destroyed is an intimate account of my journey over the last 28 years, as an above the knee amputee and as a black man living in the inner city of Philadelphia, in a community where people with disabilities are often frowned upon, ridiculed, teased, and mocked. In this project I will share with you how these experiences have shaped a quarter century of my life, how I processed through the five stages of grief and the affect it all had on me physically and emotionally.

Five Stages of Grief - Understanding the Kubler-Ross Model (psycom.net)

Denial

Denial is the stage that can initially help you survive the loss. You might think life makes no sense, has no meaning, and is too overwhelming. You start to deny the news and, in effect, go numb.

It's common in this stage to wonder how life will go on in this different state – you are in a state of shock because life as you once knew it, has changed in an instant. If you were diagnosed with a deadly disease, you might believe the news is incorrect – a mistake must have occurred somewhere in the lab–they mixed up your blood work with someone else. If you receive news on the death of a loved one, perhaps you cling to a false hope that they identified the wrong person.

In the denial stage, you are not living in 'actual reality,' rather, you are living in a 'preferable' reality. Interestingly, it is denial and shock that help you cope and survive the grief event. Denial aids in pacing your feelings of grief. Instead of becoming completely overwhelmed with grief, we deny it, do not accept it, and stagger its full impact on us at one time. Think of it as your body's natural defense mechanism saying "hey, there's only so much I can handle at once."

Once the denial and shock start to fade the healing process begins. At this point, those feelings that you were once suppressing begin making their way to the surface.

Anger

Once you start to live in 'actual' reality again and not in 'preferable' reality, anger might start to set in. This is a common stage to think "why me?" and "life's not fair!" You might look to blame others for the cause of your grief and also may redirect your anger to close friends and family. You find it incomprehensible of how something like this could happen to you. If you are strong in faith, you might start to question your belief in God. "Where is God? Why didn't He protect me?"

Researchers and mental health professionals agree that this anger is a necessary stage of grief, and encourage the anger. It's important to truly feel the anger. It is thought that even though you might seem like you are in an endless cycle of anger, it will dissipate – and the more you truly feel the anger, the more quickly it will dissipate, and the more quickly you will heal. It is not healthy to suppress your feelings of anger – it is a natural response – and perhaps, arguably, a necessary one.

In everyday life, we are normally told to control our anger toward situations and toward others. When you experience a grief event, you might feel disconnected from reality – that you have no grounding anymore. Your life has shattered and there's nothing solid to hold onto. Think of anger as a strength to bind you to reality. You might feel deserted or abandoned during a grief event. It may seem as if no one is there. You cling to the idea that you are alone in this world.

The direction of anger toward something or somebody is what might bridge you back to reality and connect you to people again. It is a "thing." It's something to grasp onto – a natural step in healing.

Bargaining

When something bad has happened, have you ever caught yourself making a deal with God? "Please God, if you heal my husband, I will strive to be the best wife I can ever be – and never complain again." This is bargaining.

In a way, this stage is false hope. You might falsely make yourself believe that you can avoid the grief through a type of negotiation. If you change this, I'll change that. You are so desperate to get your life back to how it was before the grief event, you are willing to make a major life change in an attempt toward normality.

Guilt is a common wing man of bargaining. This is when you endure the endless "what if" statements. What if I had left the house five minutes sooner – the accident would have never happened. What if I encouraged him to go to the doctor six months ago like I first thought – the cancer could have been found sooner and he could have been saved.

Depression

Depression is a commonly accepted form of grief. In fact, most people associate depression immediately with grief – as it is a "present" emotion. It represents the emptiness we feel when we are living in reality and realize the person or situation is gone or over.

In this stage, you might withdraw from life, feel numb, live in a fog, and not want to get out of bed. The world might seem too much and too overwhelming for you to face. You don't want to be around others, don't feel like talking, and experience feelings of hopelessness. You might even experience suicidal thoughts – thinking "what's the point of going on?"

Acceptance

The last stage of grief identified by Kübler-Ross is acceptance. Not in the sense that "it's okay my husband died" rather, "my husband died, but I'm going to be okay."

In this stage, your emotions may begin to stabilize. You re-enter reality. You come to terms with the fact that the "new" reality is that your partner is never coming back

– or that you are going to succumb to your illness and die soon – and you're okay with that. It's not a "good" thing – but it's something you can live with. It is definitely a time of adjustment and readjustment. There are good days, there are bad days, and then there are good days again.

In this stage, it does not mean you'll never have another bad day – where you are uncontrollably sad. But the good days tend to outnumber the bad days. In this stage, you may lift from your fog, you start to engage with friends again, and might even make new relationships as time goes on. You understand your loved one can never be replaced, but you move, grow, and evolve into your new reality.

———————————

The stage of denial will reveal moments of darkness, hatred, and pain. It will explore moments that would later define my struggle socially, as well as some vivid accounts of trying to return to a life of social interaction from a person that was naturally shy, reserved, and suffered from self-esteem issues. I secretly was devasted on the inside and unbalanced on the outside.

Upon researching the Kubler-Ross Model the clarity surfaced in my life that I was and had been dealing with the five stages of grief. I would have never acknowledged it until reading the clear definitions of each stage. Looking over the last 25+ years this is my personal understanding and journey of how each stage was revealed in my life. Although grief and loss is defined, it is also lived by each person personally. My experiences are the following defining five stages of grief and loss in my life.

The stage of anger will explore some emotional dark places that were at war with the state of my inner man, as a kindling of vengeance was fueled by the fear of rejection and the torn emotions of acceptance and fear.

The stage of depression will weave together the entanglement of denial and anger leading to isolation and feelings of abandonment while hiding truth in plain sight.

The stage of bargaining will detail the emotional insecurity of being a black man with a physical disability trying to fit into the established social norms, and how this would steer my decisions in relation to love, sex and relationships.

The stage of acceptance will forever keep me centered and at peace. There is a process of transformation of the mind. Where the message of "The Kingdom" of God is the center and all things unfold with divine purpose and intent.

Let us take this journey of a missing limb, and how the struggles stressed, stretched and strengthened me—thus leading me to overcoming.

CHAPTER ONE

LIMB LOSS, LIFE GAINED (JANUARY 20, 1993)

"A TRAGEDY BECAME A TROPHY."

The events that changed my life began, at 12:20 am Wednesday, June 20, 1993. Myself and a coworker turned onto the 5200 block of Addison Street. Bright streetlights concealed a person approaching us demanding our money. We looked at one other in disbelief that someone was standing before us with a shotgun. A sawed-off barrel shotgun aimed directly at my chest. Blast! The smell of burned flesh and blood splashed in my face. My natural reaction caused me to lunge forward and grab the gunman. Tears leaked down my face as they froze along my cheeks, lips, and chin. Lying in the cold street, I could hear fire and rescue in the distance.

Upon arriving at the Emergency Room, loud rushing sounds were piercing my ears. The doctor unzipped the black contraption that was holding my leg. I heard the doctor telling my parents that they would likely have to remove my left leg. I grappled in a faint voice," Do not cut off my leg. Let me die!" They called for an operating room and rushed me down the corridor.

I awoke around 4:00 am in this bright room with a tube inserted in my throat. Immediately I panicked and tried to remove it, but I was unable to move any parts of my body.

Sounds crowded-in all around me. Chirps. Beats, buzzers all were high pitch sounds in the room.

The nurse appeared and asked me to calm down and said that I was in a recovery room. I was moving my head in all directions trying to move my hands and body and could feel nothing except for tears flowing down my face and lips touching a plastic tube.

She said you will be going back into surgery soon. They were trying their best to save my left leg. She told me they needed to do it in stages because my blood pressure was a concern, but that we would be heading back into surgery once I was cleared.

I started to calm down although the tears were flowing heavy. The beaming lights of the room and the coldness in the air was uncomfortable. In a sway of a second, I began to feel this warm hand grasp mine and it was Ms. Barbara, one of my coworkers from McDonald's. Until this day, I have no idea how she knew about what had happened that night or how she got there. But, I surely was grateful to be holding her hand in that tragic moment.

After another surgery, it is now 11:40 am, as I awaken to the look of concern and tears on the sorrowing faces of family and friends. I was still intubated and in confinement. Medical staff was prepared for my immediate response to pull that tube out of the back of my throat.

I absolutely hated that tube. As if the pain from the surgery was not enough. It was something about that tube that made me hyper aware that I was in peril. My entire body felt numb and bloated. My lips felt as if someone had glossed them with sand and glue.

I tried to communicate that I needed some water and to please take this tube out of my throat, but I could not speak. Maybe it was a blessing I could not speak because I could not ask about my leg.

The tears began to flow, for the restraints across my body indicated to me that something was wrong. The nurse along with family convinced me to calm down and allow my pressure to stabilize. This would be the only way they would remove the tube. Dozing in and out of consciousness I tried to be present, but my emotions and the meds won every time. I had to have sedation medication to keep me stabilized and to remove the tube.

After a few hours had passed, restraints remained but the tube was removed. I immediately requested water. Much to my disappointment I was only graced with a pink sponge to wet my lips and the interior of my mouth. I asked in a small, muffled voice if they had cut off my leg and the nurse said yes. I just starting yelling in a weak voice let me die, please let me die.

The next thing I can recall is being in a regular room later that day. I believe they either sedated me more, or I simply blacked out. I hope it was the latter but most likely it was a combination of the two.

The first night was mostly the staff getting comfortable with all the questions that family and friends had and the projection of what my life would be like going forward. The reality of what would be my norm was unknown in that first twenty-four hours. The pain medication had me in a state of ambivalence and numbness.

The next day the surgical team arrived around 6am and prepared me for an additional removal of the residual limb due to the gunshot pellets that were still in the limb. It was about five hours later that an operating room opened, and they transported me to the place where I would lose yet another piece of myself.

It was another two hours before the actual surgery would take place. I arrived back to my room around 6:00 pm, and the medical staff had informed me of the list of names of persons that had come to visit or called to check on me. I know there were many conversations on that day waiting to go into surgery, but honestly, I do not have any recall of such.

The third day presented its first challenges. It was the first time that I experienced the sensation of what was described to me later as *"Phantom Pain."* Phantom pain is pain that feels like it is coming from a body part that is no longer there. Doctors once believed this post-amputation phenomenon was a psychological problem, but experts now recognize that these real sensations originate in the spinal cord and brain.

The jolt of force that creates this phantom pain can only, in my case, be comparable to putting your togue on a nine-volt battery. The next eighteen days in the hospital required five additional operations. I clinically died three times during that twenty-one day stay. The shock and trauma caused night sweats and would require dry linen changes during the night every thirty minutes or so. This is still present in my life today. I must sleep with towels underneath me or the bed and linens become a pool of sweat. At times, my temperature rises to levels where you can literally see vapors as steam is released from my body.

The wound care after each operation, the drains, catheters, night sweats, constipation, and a missing limb were all overwhelming. The blood thinners, the blood transfusions, the pressure medication, an IV Morphine drip, Tylenol, Percocet, Motrin, and Advil dictated my life for days.

During the day, I was grateful for all the visitors, phone calls etc. but at night there was a level of suffering that I endured that I am finally ready to talk about. Seeing my leg blow up in front of me repeatedly was terrifying. The thoughts of death were present every night. I was afraid that every time I closed my eyes would be the last. The unclear image of the dude that shot me was unbearable. Every time someone would enter the room the grip of fear was present. The future seemed to be a waste of time. I was not sure I would survive the present moment.

There were many people that helped me to cope with just wanting to continue. The smooth vocals of the one and only Anita Baker comforted me when the phones shut off in the wee hours of each night. I welcomed the brightness of the sun each morning for it was a sign that life was still present.

My mom wiped me down with that good ole green alcohol after each surgery. This helped with the fevers and trauma of it all. I know she got that advice from my grandma, and it surely worked. Her caress kept us connected. Through this experience our bond grew deeper. I witnessed the weight of concern behind her eyes grow heavier every time she blinked. Yet, it was her faith that undoubtedly pierced the windows of my soul.

The timbre of travail in my father's voice echoed off the hollow walls of the hospital room and nestled beside me in my confinement. This tiny bed was both my prison and my protection. Still, dad was steadfast. But, did he even believe the words, "everything will be alright," that he whispered faintly to me?

After twenty-one days in the hospital, and seven operations it was finally discharge day. No time to adjust because in just two days I was readmitted to the hospital due to morphine addiction. The next four days I spent on the detox unit; placed on a clear liquid diet. The first 48 hours were torture, constant fever, and vomiting.

Once back home, the goal was to get back to work while waiting on my first prosthesis fitting. I was discharged with a prescription for 800mgs of Motrin as needed. Little did they know that the need was every two to three hours. Any missed dosage caused the pain to be unbearable.   Over time that level of usage increased to dangerous levels.

The residual limb: what remained of my left leg-a quarter length of my other thigh, finally started to heal and shape itself, and the discovery of a lack of muscle tissue in my back thigh area was noticeable. The damaged muscle tissue left my left side weak and hollow. There was no muscle tissue to develop an excellent walking pattern.

Many efforts to compensate for the lack of muscle tissue failed, causing a gross gait pattern. Months of therapy did not help correct the issue. My walking pattern was like a black creature dragging itself out of the shadows. Sometimes I wanted to fade into those shadows. Anything not to be different. It was so uncomfortable, painful, and embarrassing, and for many years my twisted body left me using a cane.

I returned to college in the fall semester of 1993 soon after getting adjusted to my first prothesis. I was welcomed as a person of strength for overcoming a tragedy (with hidden addictions). For the first time, I was away from the support system that kept its eye on the now disfigured black man. What a sucker I was for allowing this to happen and survived.

The campus life took its toll: the walking of distances, the urge to be social, and the need to fit in created more distress. Everyone seemed to block out the fact that I had a missing limb. I somehow became more social than previously. It was like the limb loss provided an entrance of acceptance or was it sympathy?

My active involvement created expectations that my body could not handle. I was an active member of many organizations on campus in various roles with the student government. My activities included being on the road broadcasting football games, coaching the intramural basketball dream team to the championship, leading, and directing the gospel choir, and mentoring incoming first-year students.

I experienced daily challenges. I often missed classes, and some days would only get up to eat in the cafeteria. The acceptance of strangers was welcoming. It felt good to be around folks who did not know my struggles.

I explored all facets of life in those college days. The people, places, and experiences will forever impact my life. I received acceptance from those who were not afraid to live life by their own rules. The fear of rejection grew in what was the mainstream society. The vicious hatred manifested in separations and experiences of not mixing my associations. The addiction increased more and more.

At the time of graduation, the dosage of pain medication was insurmountable and abusive. I even tried other forms of pain relief, but nothing worked like my pills. More people. More places. More popularity. More pain. More problems. More pills.

The day and night of my graduation was a difficult feat. The distance from the far end of the library on campus to my seat inside the original football field was unbearable. My pride would not and could not accept that I was a disabled person. I just wanted the day to be magical. My immediate family and the women that stood by me during this ordeal were present. All seemed like a fairytale until the phantom pain quickly caused my magical day to fade as the pain traveled throughout my lower back and legs.

The party that night was simultaneously honoring and painful. At the end of the night, after making sure everyone got home, my world erupted into tears. Shards of salted liquid raced down my face onto my pillow like the rushing storm waters that overtake dams. My emotions overwhelmed me and manifested as a flood of crying. What was ahead was my hidden addiction, despair, the development of separation, and my plunge into the depths of the unknown.

After attending a new employee orientation, the next few weeks I started my professional career at Children's Hospital of Philadelphia. The following eleven years, there would be many "challenges and opportunities" to present themselves, as one of my coworkers would always tell me. I will never forget the amazing people of color who helped mold and shape my successful journey. I am grateful to the chefs, cooks, cashiers, patient service staff, utility staff, vending staff, catering staff, housekeepers, customers, and management team. My success was motivated by them each day. I heard their stories, heeded their suggestions, and held fast to their criticisms. The journey from washing lettuce at the back sink to becoing a director responsible for a five-million-dollar foodservice operation was phenomenal.

My journey later transported me to the School District of Philadelphia Headquarters, the liaison for a third-party contractor, directing the housekeeping staff for the next seven years.

The building's massive square footage as a housekeeping director systematically increased the usage of pain medications. I directed an all-African American staff; what an experience. The politics and the position were interesting in those days. The culture within the black culture is impressive. The uniqueness of my people is breathtaking.

The years to follow led me back to a management position again at McDonald's and Jos A Banks. My disability finally caused me to retire from the hospitality and service industry in December of 2014. Approximately 21 years later- another cycle of 3 dimensions of completion. I am currently giving back to my community mentoring adults with learning challenges and autism, working on myself, and my addiction. My direction has influenced me to live.

EVEN AFTER THE FINAL CUTS, I AM STILL REALIZING THAT GOD WAS NOT TAKING AWAY. GOD WAS MAKING A WAY. THE CUTTING OF MY LEG WAS A TRAGEDY. THE CARVING OF MY LIFE IS CREATING A TROPHY.

CHAPTER TWO

I CAN'T BELIEVE THIS HAS HAPPENED TO ME!
(DENIAL STAGE)

This stage challenged me physically because I was not prepared to live a life without a limb. The process of getting an artificial limb was supposed to replace the limb that was amputated. The medical professionals gave me a false sense of hope that the limb replacement would provide me with the same quality of life.

They referred me to articles and information about walking, running, and living a smooth everyday life after limb loss. The fact that I am an above-the-knee amputee is not easy, mainly because there is no natural knee function. The prosthesis for an above-the-knee amputee cannot bend at the knee, leading to the inability to walk and run, coupled with no muscle tissue mass in the residual limb area. This news left me disappointed and angry when I discovered that I would not function and walk in a typical fashion as the doctors had led me to believe I would.

At first, the prosthesis caused me to have irregular walking patterns. I realized that I looked like a person who was learning to walk after suffering a stroke. A stroke victim often appears to walk as if they are dragging one side of their body. The struggle to walk generally led to years of embarrassment. I was used to dancing, running ball, running, leaping, and all manners of physical activity.

What young black virile man would want to be viewed as less than? Walking in front of people made me feel uncomfortable and ashamed of my disability, and it often caused me to withdraw from people. I was frightened by my disfigurement. It brought anger and insecurities, which led me to overcompensate in many areas of my life. I tried to mask my disappointment for allowing this to happen to me.

I struggled daily knowing there should have been a different outcome that night.

I lived with daily frustration for not taking control of the scene that night, knowing that everyone would have walked away without any injuries if I had done so. I know that given a few seconds, I would have been able to convince this young guy to take whatever possessions and go. This fear developed into many acts of rage within me. Daily I found myself asking, "how the fuck did I let this happen to me?" For the first time, I found myself no longer wanting to be Teto Saunders. This rage began to manifest a hardcore thug mentality, and I wanted to take vengeance against everyone that made me feel ashamed by the way they looked at me.

I worked in fast-food restaurants for many years, and during fits of rage, I often wanted to grab someone by their throat and beat the shit out of them during a heated encounter. While in these fits of rage, I began to see hints of my inherited anger develop within me; it had me feeling very conflicted. The imagery of violent rages beating persons into submission for my own inferior fear of rejection. Afraid to commit to serious relationships due to the flashes of terror not manifested but conscious in my thoughts.

My parents had just reconciled during this incident. The feeling of now no longer being the man of the house and the limb loss was getting to me. I recall one day the fear overtook me, and out of complete anger, I hit someone upside the head with a fire extinguisher and felt little to almost no remorse. I faked it to keep my job, but I felt some sense of vengeance against anyone ever trying to take advantage of me again. Grace was on my side that day.

The denial of dealing with the truth led me to purchase a gun. The gun gave me security because I would kill or harm anyone that caused me to fear. I got a license to carry it openly and wore it in public with a sense of pride, waiting for someone to fuck with me.

I wanted the person that harmed me that night to turn a corner and see me standing there with a gun in my hands, and ultimately cause them to experience the same fear I felt on that night, as my life was fading away from me. You have no idea what it feels like to know you are dying, and the shock your body goes into trying to stop the feeling of what you know is the end of your earthly existence.

I would often see the dark specks of the person that shot me in other people. I never had a clear visual image of him in my head. I wanted vengeance no matter who it was. People made me uncomfortable and fearful.

It was leading to a deeper denial instead of dealing with my internal pain. I started to develop a relationship with those the world would call "thugs." I would witness the deplorable conditions that they some lived in. It made sense why so many of them had a challenging personality. Everything would cause me to be angry at my upbringing and the struggle we endured, often causing me to pull my gun out and threaten people, knowing I was too afraid to pull the trigger, let alone harm someone.

The experience of their lives helped me in the years to come. I was advised never to walk in a new hood with my head down and always look people in their eyes and prick their souls to cause respect. I was told never to let anyone know you were fearful because that gave them an immediate advantage.

It took me back to the times as a teenager when playing sports and learning from my uncles never to show weakness or fear. I was taught to shoot the basketball, go up for the rebound, throw with determination, catch with confidence, throw with accuracy, and hit with power. I was able to develop at my own pace. I always knew a gang would come to my rescue or defend me at any time.

My thoughts focused on how this could have happened after knowing that fear had been conquered but now returned. Childhood feelings of always being called different from everyone else, always the odd one would find its way into my heart. A loner, in many ways, I enjoyed the silence of the world. I recall being directed or obligated to be involved in sports and outside activities growing up. I was self-taught; all the rules and how to officiate all sports. Due to low interest in some sports, I was often left to officiate and referee; I made efforts to overcome that by playing many sports later in life. Now it felt like a reversal of time had taken place, and there again arose conflicted feelings.

The denial of dealing with that conflict caused behaviors that created shame. These behaviors were frowned upon, and the things I would often hear from a child's perspective from adults, especially towards our family members cause, instant shame, and withdrawn feelings. To hear how people thought about others whom they loved was conflict within itself. Often hearing adult's conversation about the future of members of the family based on their character. The women were often called naïve for allowing subpar men to be in their lives and create life. The men were applauded for not allowing themselves to settle for one woman. The detailed description of those failed relationships that were engrossed in physical and emotional abuse was somehow accepted. It led to a denial of emotions; I was ashamed to be different. This young black man was now odd and strange.

One day I overheard a painful conversation about how some of my family felt about me. They simply said, I would turn out like my father. The fear of being a negative topic of adult conversation scared me. I developed a thirst for knowledge of things we had in common, and I created a profound response to those subjects. My voice was finally being heard. I started mastering numbers and figures. I became attracted to gambling, which gave me control and respect. Control was something I did not have on January 20, 1993. The development of ways to "win at all costs" set in. I was good at it, and sometimes too good. It made me a target for stick-up kids. I often caused trauma and sparked fear that led my mind to visualize their presence and switch up my routine. Later in life, this development would open doors for me in my professional and ministry endeavors. The ability to calculate and assume movement proves to work for me in managing multi-million-dollar operations.

The fear of seeing anyone victimized caused me to connect with others who could not defend themselves—often getting urgent calls to come to their defense with my weapon to scare off any threats. I kept a gun by my side for over ten years. More recently I recovered after an incident in which authorities removed my gun from my home. Still, I never reclaimed it. It would lead to someone's death and physical imprisonment, which I was already living, daily proof of what could happen if I spiraled into a dark place; a place where my fear and rage turned into manipulating people, places, and things. If I did not have my leg to walk into places, I desired I would surely use my mind, persuasion, and craftiness to get what I wanted.

The denial stage revealed many concerns about my brokenness. Being often overshadowed by love, bondage, brokenness, lies, truth, right, wrong, fair, and just; I finally would get to a balanced mental, physical, and spiritual life that led to healing, restoration, and strength to overcome every obstacle before me.

I HAVE CALCULATED THE EVOLUTION OF MY DENIAL.
EMBARRASSED. ENGROSSED. ENDANGERED. EMBRACED. EMPOWERED.

I felt embarrassed and became engrossed in activities that endangered my life. But, once I embraced my reality, the truth empowered me to move on to the next step.

CHAPTER THREE

UNHINGED
(THE STAGE OF ANGER)

This stage was internal, and I desired to get even with the unknown. The removal of my limb was always on my mind. The visions of seven operations that chopped more of my leg haunted me, daily. I imagined my leg shrinking and my life fading away, daily. How would I age and cope with a limb loss? I could never again experience the joy of walking the beach, roller skating, playing any sports, or just standing in the shower without the fear of falling.

The imagery grew more intense over time, and there seemed to be no relief of blocking out these visions. The anger had me starting to question everything in my life. I started to doubt my future. I did not see myself living beyond established milestones. I began to withdraw slowly from my established circles of family and friends. I began to convince myself that they only remained connected due to pity. I told myself they were dragging me along because of the advantages of being young with a car, influence, and a needy shy person. They needed me as much as I thought I needed them. The thought of people using me was a conflict in my head, for as much as it appeared, they had the advantage.

The feelings of hatred rose out of anger. One day while in a work environment, there was an incident involving a racial slur. The outburst led to an investigation yielding not in my favor. Instead of complaining, the anger told me to "get even," which was my mission. The doctors ordered me to take time off, and I used that time to plot my next move. They saw it as punishment. I saw it as an opportunity to strike and strike hard.

I decided to return to work knowing that there was a lawsuit against them for violating my ability to work due to disability. The atmosphere was strange to me, and there was no consideration for my disability. I was mistreated due to my incapacity and inability to keep up with the workflow. I often stretched myself beyond my physical ability to prove some self-worth.

It was early in my limb loss, and the physical demands were overwhelming. I started to take pain medication in large doses to cope with the pain because the only way to support myself was to work. I could take three to four 800mgs of medicine at one time. It truly numbed the pain and all feelings. In the early days of my disability, the government denied my application for social security and social security disability.

Their decision only increased the volume of pain medication used for a workday. The mood swings ripped my insides, there were days when I just did not have the ability to move let alone work but, the pain medication gave me the ability to remain professional. I was often numb and lacked emotions.

It increased over time from one pain pill every four hours to multiple within that time frame. It was clear that my body was no longer able to function without the medication. When the drug was not available, the anger turned to aggression, leaving me isolated. I had quickly, suddenly evolved into a functional addict.

I would often take breaks to the restroom to massage the limb, hoping to ease the pain. It would work sometimes, and other times I increased my medication intake. I kept a First Aid Kit accessible to address open wounds and skin irritation. The design of the prosthesis and my irregular gate caused daily skin breakdown. In the beginning, the process of wearing the prosthesis required a lotion substance on my skin and the hard plastic surface of the limb—most days applying the lotion several times to avoid skin breakdown.

It was embarrassing and angering when others would notice blood on my clothes from the skin bleeding from irritation. One day, I heard a young child pointing and saying that man was walking funny and bleeding. I would get so angry for allowing this to happen. I would often want to walk off the job, but then I would have to walk in front of people judging me. Getting a paycheck to be an object of pity was better than sitting at home becoming more detached.

Looking back at the age of 15, I was allowed to attend Drexel University Upward Bound program because of my competitive academic nature. I was also a wrestling fan, and I copied the personalities of several of the icons of my era. I was the perfect beard of the four horsemen. The ability to merge all their signature moves into one performance was magical. It made me no longer feel shy or weak. I had mastered a persona that took me to the height of euphoria. If only I could embody that persona now would my disability disappear, and I be seen as I once was?

I was just angry internally all the time. I could no longer do the things that made me feel secure within myself. The desire to never fail would have been throwing tennis balls outside on the front steps or a side way around the way to master the split-finger fast ball, curve ball, and the mystical knuckle ball striking out the side to win the world series. It would be in the basement with a broom and tennis ball shooting the winning goal in hockey. I would have one of my sisters holding the tip of the football as the winning field goal soared through the uprights of the end zone. Then, to the last second half court shot to win the NBA championship. I could no longer do any of those things. These dreams would never become my realities. I truly believed that one day I would be a walk on at any of the major sports and become a star. I had to settle for just being an avid fan.

Competitiveness in college covered my anger; few may remember those track days at Widener University. I developed late in athletics but also gave it my all when playing sports. I was not good at playing with skilled athletes; however, I held my own in junior varsity and interleague sports. I would have been successful at the division three-level, and then the limb loss transpired. I was competitive all my life in some fashion or another.

I had to discover that feeling again in college, where my world was never constant. You could meet someone in one semester, and the next, they are never to be seen. Also, I fell in love quickly and yearned for affection. I was afraid of commitment from the experience of abandonment in relationships. The expression of anger, violence, and disappointment was often seen and felt in my heart and mind. I was angry at myself for having a fear of those emotions. Life experiences should have driven the opposite effects, but they induced more fear and anger.

These emotions are still evident in my life today, which inspired this book. I started going to the gym for weightlifting, and many days envisioned myself running; often, one could find me on the basketball court. This competitive nature made me feel whole and complete. At times, the gym centered my life, and things were at peace. I would rediscover this passion later in life.

The anger of losing my limb and the desire for a sexual relationship, and the unknown reactions to removing an artificial limb before sex were emotionally overwhelming. It led to many uncomfortable moments. The desire for physical intimacy was replaced with pornographic images and led to a desire for porn and self-pleasuring. I would discover that many never asked why I had a limp. I would be angry when people would be close to me and be uncomfortable when seeing the process of detachment. I would get angry because the question was not asked and that I did not share.

At times, I would often direct the probing of my body to spark a conversation that created comfortability or caused some to be more uncomfortable. It never stopped the sex, though; maybe some of my sex partners were simply curious, perhaps some just freaky. I never felt comfortable with the limb. It was awkward to attach and embarrassing to remove. There were moments during the multiple surgeries that the function of my male reproductive system was numb. I recall those moments required a direct conversation with God.

During that time, I was only committed to earning income—relationships developed in helping others with their life struggles. The anger within my community increased over time, experiencing the depth of pain associated with broken or single-parent homes. Despair forged friendships forever. The bond is forever unbreakable. I cannot begin to list names here, for they know my place in their hearts. To the people who are near and dear to my heart, the struggle is real, but we are overcoming it every day. I will never give up on them. And, I trust that the covenant commitment is mutual. They will not give up one me. More importantly, neither of us can give up on ourselves. The strange way our pain directed us to meet in the past will be our painful testimony of conquering and winning in the days, weeks, months and years to come.

The anger of abandonment and disappointment can often only bc undcrstood within. Our outward cxprcssion would never reveal the origins of that emotion. The rage is the outward fight of that internal emotion that you cannot seem to correct. It can hinder relationships, stunt your growth, pause your progress, and victimize you from success.

You will measure your success by the depth of your failures. You see the justification in your actions because it is as damning as your last failure. You will continuously engage in misdeeds and blame the negligence of others for correcting yours.

The anger never seems to lessen but becomes more evident when things are not going your way. The inability for others to accept their presence alone fuels that internal anger of disappointment and abandonment. The absence of their responsibility to assist in your healing process increases the damage to oneself.

I still deal with waves of anger even now fueled by my inability to do the things that once were natural. The inability to run, skateboard, play sports, stick my feet in the ocean is frustrating. These daily struggles to overcome this level of anger drives my pursuit of happiness in other areas.

ANGER IS NOT AN ISSUE. IT IS THE ACTIONS WE ATTACH TO IT THAT COMPLICATE OUR LIVES. ANGER IN ACTION IS RAGE.
WHEN WE CAGE THE RAGE, WE CAN MOVE TO THE NEXT STAGE.

CHAPTER FOUR

NOT IN THE HOOD
(THE STAGE OF DEPRESSION)

Depression not a sign of mental illness; it is the appropriate response to a significant loss. You might experience intense sadness, decreased sleep, reduced appetite, and loss of motivation.

I suffered from a low level of depression that began with New Birth Fellowship Tabernacle Church's birthing on March 28, 2004.

March 28, 2004 was the New Birth Fellowship Tabernacle Church launch under my leadership; the appearance of a high-profile presence led to a stage of depression. I had convinced myself that my flesh would catch up with my spirit. It would take eleven years for this to become a reality. The depressive mindset took time to develop and time to reverse. It progressed over time, especially during uncertain times. I subconsciously learned to isolate myself inwardly and outwardly. I became visibly invisible to myself and others.

Sundays in my life were for church, and it was a contrast to the hustle and chaos in my professional and personal personas. The Fellowship Tabernacle Church was where being odd was expected; where weekly gatherings of people from all sectors of life took place.

I didn't feel like an awkward person among so many various personalities. I blended in well and noticed during my disability, it didn't seem to cause people to be uncomfortable. There was no feeling of eyes watching me. People talked to me without prior knowledge of the life led when I had both lower limbs, before I lost my limb, and limped through life. It was fantastic to be at a place of discovery of what was instead of what had been.

The development of my relationship with God matured in June of 1996. I had many more years of church experiences, but never the relationship that developed after college. I witnessed my friend William O. Burney, Sr's life end. It shook my life forever. It was as if I was living outside my body, watching myself die. As he was in critical condition, the hospital scene took a toll on every young person at the ministry. It not only was an awakening emotionally but spiritually. We excelled in a different place. The bond that developed amongst the peers he grew up in the church with was tight. They now were my new support system.

I found a place even more in the ministry because of William's death. We would discover later that his girlfriend was pregnant. Yvette Young, "Mrs. Toot," gave birth to his son William O. Burney, Jr. on February 17, 1997. I promised myself that his son would not know the emotion of not having a father. To this day, I have been fully present and entirely active in his life.

Later in ministry, my son, Cornelius James Daye, came along. His high level of energy was often too much for people to handle. For some reason, he bonded with me and would instantly calm himself in my presence. Now, adults bring him to me in distress, and he would quickly calm himself, and we were able to hang out. At the age of fourteen, his mom asked me to care for him full-time.

The one that has my name is Leonard Teto Purnell. He is the brother of Yolanda Johnson-Jenkins, who was my sister Kisha Evans's best friend growing up. On January 23, 1993, he was born in the same hospital, so Yolanda asked her mother to name him after me, so she agreed to name him after his father and myself. His father died early in his life, and I accepted that parental role. The perfect trio was complete Leonard (Lenny), Cornelius (Neil), and William (Lil Will).

Once, the ministry of Fellowship Tabernacle moved to North Carolina. I experienced gaps in my established Christian experience. I was able to fade away to my home church weekly after having my services. The stress and pressure were re-lived each week by experiencing my place of acceptance and comfortability. I became isolated all over again out of fear.

The fear of being alone, although surrounded by people every day, caused me to withdraw. I was able to function with a purpose only. If there was a need or a goal, it filled my time and helped me avoid the emptiness. Somehow being a busybody gave meaning to my life. The progression of isolation transpired over time. There were times when things were aligned in my life. However, a sense of feeling needed, desired, and encouraged faded in my relationships, not just in my personal life but in ministry. When the two seemed to interconnect, the fear of being alone and rejected intensified. These moments of intensity were terrifying.

My escape was work. There was no disclosure of my personal life at times. I would only tell a few selected people about my life outside of work. The age of social media didn't help keep it undisclosed for any length of time. The moment that people will say, "are you Elder, Pastor, Bishop Saunders," and then I would have to shift my response. Often, the feeling of shame would overcome me. To advocate for my coworkers was just too much to overcome—the behaviors of some in the workplace professionally. The unbelievable stuff that people with status (based on a skill set or some favoritism) was shocking regarding how they viewed my coworkers. Often awkward moments at a future meeting and encountered with those professionals who once talked openly in my presence.

Those who were my direct reports would be surprised by how once angered customers would calm down in my presence. Most of the time, it was not a black person they were expecting to respond, especially one with a disability. Shame was upon many of them as they would see me often struggle to walk the 10,000 square feet from the nearest elevator to their cubicle or office to discover there was no sense of urgency. I would offer my direct office line and email for any concerns. My presence lessened the overall complaints, but this led to other management methods to tarnish my hourly coworkers, with technical violations that led to many wasted attempts at distinct actions that led to unfavorable decisions.

I would make it back to my office many days after walking miles and just wanted to take my toys and go home. I could not believe this was my current job. The blessing was that the job was an actual Monday to Friday 8:00 am to 4:00 pm gig. Covering the day shift gave me the flexibility to have a balanced life. The ability to travel freely with no restrictions was a perk for sure. The time was spent mainly at Allied Prothesis, seeking help with the walking demands of the job. There were three prostheses designed during those years, all led to constant skin breakdowns and increased phantom pain from daily walking. More and more medications were needed, I was willing to try anything to relieve that pain.

The downward spiral increased over the years, with increased isolation. The yearning to escape birthed a season where we had four services a day to satisfy my need to reduce my isolation. It worked for a season, and things were growing by leaps and bounds in all areas of my life. It was not sustainable in the long run. It was just too much for the ministry to commit to, although my shattered self was all ready to see what this would create.

The scale back once again increased the isolation and fear of rejection. Seeing my recovery's vision shortened led to spending time with folks who were just as broken as me and inwardly fighting within the ministry to protect me from myself. Yes, I acknowledge that some of my developed associates were not fruitful. But the established ones were just as broken and one-sided. The disconnect of manipulating my time, talent, and treasure led to packing up their tents and fleeing. It caused me to develop a three-day rule. Within the established three days, whatever caused the issues, had that time frame to recover or "kick rocks."

Some of my associations were just pleasing to the flesh. It was pleasing to be motivating people to a better moral standard, yet aware it was only most times momentary in their lives. I often fell into that mindset; it was grace that would help me overcome my sins. Taking for granted the mercy that was extended. The constant repeating of one's sins can take its toll. I found myself wandering in my own wilderness. My spiritual parent was miles away, and the tension between my spiritual brothers and sisters led to division and jealousy.

We fought for the saints' attention, leaving all of us scattered and unable to support or trust each other. The anger that develops at the rejection of my once co-laborers was ever-present. I tried to understand their views on things, but it always was related to my experience. No one forced you into anything. You ministry endeavors have been done willfully. I justified my actions by saying we did it consciously.

Years later, it is still divided over things that should have united us. Yet, we always smile at each other's accomplishments in secret. One day we will not have to admire each other from afar but will be united in Spirit, with love and compassion. Aware of each unique challenge and perspective of ministry cannot be mature enough to heal but remain ill. Rejection is absolute and grips so many with fear. The constant fear of rejection is deep-rooted in so many of us. We mask it and never allow it to come to the surface.

If it rises to the surface, others may identify it and cause a confirmation that can lead to healing. The fear of rejection hinders self-growth. Awareness brings about Acknowledgement. Acknowledgement creates confirmation. And, confirmation can ultimately—eventually—lead to recovery. The freeing of one's bound soul is healing to those who are hurting.

DEPRESSION WAS NOT A SICKNESS OR A WEAKNESS FOR ME.
DEPRESSION WAS THE EXPRESSION THAT LEFT ME WITH THE
IMPRESSION THAT A CHANGE WAS NECESSARY.

CHAPTER FIVE

NOTHING SEEMED NORMAL
(THE STAGE OF BARGAINING)

Having confidence growing up was like the old handheld device called Etch a Sketch. One would spend time creating images that could disappear in seconds. I wanted to hold on to those images for a while before they were wiped clean. Things just were not always permanent in those days.

I was born on Friday the 13th. The year was 1970. My mother was 20 years old when she gave birth to a tiny tike named Teto. It was quite a testament of resilience to have celebrated my fiftieth birthday amidst a global pandemic and a country divided against itself in social upheaval and racial injustice. Interesting how closely reminiscent of my own life the world looked in 2020. Unclear of the destination, I would be remiss to say it had not been quite the journey.

Life has a way of spinning you into a circular motion of twists and turns that can hurt, heal, help, hinder, and take you to the brink of not knowing yourself at times. This constant movement shaped my life. The feeling of insecurity and confidence was at the hands of others most of my life. Others defined my life stages based on their insecurities and trust, and I was sometimes drawn to others who seemed just like myself, which was often comforting and sickening at the same time.

My childhood was typical concerning my immediate family. We were tight-knit; there were eleven aunts and uncles on my mom's side of the family. I was raised in a multiple generational "setting." For years there was no distinction between my mom and grand mom. Some of my aunts and uncles were only a few years older than me, the same age as me, or a bit younger. My mom was referred to by her nickname "Lennie." We called my Beloved grandmother "mom" or "mommy," and we adapted that unspoken awareness. Decades later, we still echo those exact words.

The spoken rule of "what happens in this house stays in this house" was the implied rule to all of us. Many things occurred in the house that were, and will forever be, secrets in those houses' walls. The documented issues of family dynamics were not unique to my family. Life experiences about trust, sexual conduct, religion, money, criminal activities, death, and physical-emotional abuse were a part of my upbringing. Many discussions of dysfunctional behaviors were often the topic of grown folk's conversations, leading to shame and exclusion.

I found myself continually having to adjust to fit into many environments. Aware of the accusations clouded in truth, yet afraid to say what, how, and why. I was internally feeling responsible based on the flaws of others. I desired others' compassion and companionship at a young age, which left me confused and inquiring about odd things. I developed an attraction to adult pornography. Interracial and violent graphic presentations drew my attention. I would search for nude content, watch daytime television glued to its sexual explicitness. My youth and teenage years were too confusing. Having the desire for love yet having sex created more confusion. I developed an eye or a sense of what was pleasurable. I would desire to be in back allies, abandoned building having girls on their knees pleasing me orally. The desire to please myself replaced those actual acts.

The fear of disease should have kept me from being sexually active, but it did not. The thrill of the conquest was more appealing than any disease. My first trip to the doctor was fourteen years old, having unprotected sex with a thirteen-year -old, but she was thick and experienced. She quickly came to realize that "it was about to go down." Thankfully, it was the least of the possible infections and was cleared up quickly.

It was one of many wild sexual experiences in my life. The normal exploration of sex came for me at such an early age; it triggered sexual desires. My exploration of sex was driven by thoughts, desires, and fantasies connected to those early experiences. I was often conflicted within myself regarding what was causing that desire. It seemed like my desires would shift quickly out of boredom. Once the conquest was completed to get my desired outcome, it wouldn't last out of boredom or sexual hunger. The experiences at my young age left me wanting a heightened sexual experience. The appetite increased during times of disappointing sexual experiences. It aligned itself with my inability to commit wholeheartedly to anyone.

It was the hidden, driven force behind all my failed relationships. Through many sexual experiences, my partners could not fulfill my emotional and physical desires; no one could align with those needs. It was always unbalanced. There was a lack in them, and there was so much insufficient in me. I often found myself begging for what was missing that would make me whole. My childhood fears would often manipulate me into investing in trying to love something that was incapable of loving me back. I never experienced any consistency in relationships. As quickly as the cravings came, so did the closure of any possibility of longevity.

Seeking that satisfaction, coupled with the loss of my limb, was often embarrassing and shameful. The awkward moments of removing the prosthesis would cloud my thoughts and leave the moments unsatisfying. I was often ashamed to want my desires met and quickly got to that climax, not concerned with others' desires. I would often think to myself, " let me get to this fast and get this prosthesis back on before any swellings developed, and the prosthesis would not fit properly without challenges." I cannot express the level of emotions I would reach when the prosthesis would not reattach without complications.

I am not able to prove this, but the blood transfusions somehow changed me, and the desire for sexual activity often made me push beyond my limb loss. I somehow changed and developed an increased sexual passion. Those passions led me into situations that were thrilling and often dangerous. Nonetheless, still attracted to the limited attention and affection led to years of self-pity and doubt, never feeling wanted or needed. Repetitive actions over the years all led to loneliness and the increased spreading of the internal void within me. I was seeking validation from persons that were seeking validation from me.

Those who looked beyond my physical disability didn't seem genuine. At the time, somehow, I could not accept that the attraction was natural. I often, at that point, had to admit that I was ashamed of my very existence. At times potential lovers would confess their love for me, and I would be stone-faced. Yearning to see myself from their perspective. Seeing myself from the reflection on their eyes would cause the shaking my head without moving it in disgrace. Saying to myself, "what are they looking at? This guy is not attractive and has a missing leg." What do you see that he is not seeing?

The constant fear of rejection caused me to stay longer than my original reservation. I compromised my happiness for others. Most of my needs were based on attention, and once you lost my attention, you lost your purpose for that space and time.

After all the surgeries in 1996, 1998, 2001, 2002, 2004, 2006, 2015, 2018; they all kept me in a state of feeling no progression. I always had this faint image of me walking, running, and living with my previous limb. Having to adjust to removing an artificial limb daily and all the sores, scars, blemishes, and pain seems unfair in the altered reality of my mind.

I walked with a limp. I walked without a limb. My faith failed. My flesh failed. It was only my fear that failed not. My limp was both physical and metaphysical. I was struggling to live a life of balance. I was failing. I had a wide gait and I could not stride my own weight. I was limping through life.

My lower half was less than half. It seemed as if every situation I walked into only got half of me. I often wandered, wondering what was missing. But, along this journey I was beginning to realize I was missing a limb. Not a body part, but an essential connection with the deepest parts of my self. My soul. My flesh was feeding me and my fears were fueling me. I needed to get a hold of my missing parts.

NOTHING SEEMED NORMAL BECAUSE I WAS NOT NORMAL. MY JOURNEY WAS MORE THAN ORDINARY, BECAUSE I AM EXTRAORDINARY.

CHAPTER SIX

KINGDOM PARADIGM
(THE STAGE OF ACCEPTANCE)

In Kingdom there exists a collective consciousness. The understanding and embrace of a paradigm where there is nothing missing, nothing lacking, nothing broken, and nothing out of place.

Acceptance is where one accepts the way things have happened and begins to start again.

The stage of acceptance will forever keep me centered and at peace—transforming the mind. The Bible contains the message of "The Kingdom," where God is the center and all things are unfolding with divine purpose and intent.

I had been in a spiritual role for fifteen years but was struggling with isolation and loneliness. I led a local ministry, worked multiple jobs, raised children, indulged in complicated relationships, and my limb loss was always on my mind. I was overwhelmed and seeking attention from anything and anyone.

Who would have known that on Saturday, September 13th, 2014, that this would be the day I would wake up in an isolated state. I sent a message via social media to the one person I had been avoiding for at least a year after initial contact. I did not know how he would respond to my request to start working out at the gym as my personal trainer and I had never really talked openly about my disability.

During my college years, I would often fade away to the weight-lifting room at the gym, usually just among strangers, seeking to improve themselves. At those times, I was at peace with myself, knowing that the only thing between me and success was my strength.

After college, I never considered being accepted in the mainstream gym. My body was increasingly becoming weaker and weaker. The steady increase in pain medication, the stress of ministry, fatherhood, professional challenges, and my pursuit of happiness all came into clear focus after just a few weeks of working out again. The response to the inbox message was short and direct. I asked, "Are you able to modify a workout routine for me with my leg?" The answer was, "For sure, come on down, and let's get this work."

I got up and purchased some workout gear that morning. I got a pair of sneakers even though I had not worn sneakers in twenty years. I bought a few shirts and some sweatpants, and my heart was pounding for the next sixty hours.

That Sunday morning, my spiritual life changed, as my natural course was about to as well. The message was entitled "I am Yet Alive." It was apparent that the acceptance process within my mind and spirit was on a collision course with destiny.

I arrived at the gym that Monday afternoon, nervous and not knowing what to expect. After the catch-up with my new personal trainer, he was already in a group training session, he quickly put me to work thru an intensive evaluation that had me gasping for air at times and losing my balance. After about an hour of attempting to do various exercises, the session was over, and it was a relief. I think the shock of the twist and turns had me walking out numb and wanting to collapse. I got home and soaked my body with witch hazel, green alcohol, and Epsom salt for over an hour.

I woke up the next morning feeling excited and was thinking of nutritional options for the day. I honestly did not know how long this energy and enthusiasm would last. I was generally frightened to walk into the gym daily but excited to get there. This excitement caused internal conflicts and often gave rise to a loss of focus during the first few months.

On many of my work out days I would sense eyes watching me from afar. I understand that my inability to balance myself was concerning to many of my fellow gym goers. Having to leave the gym soaked from the sweat of working out and having to drive home because of my subconscious fear of taking off my prosthesis to shower was demoralizing at times.

Once during an intense workout my prosthesis slipped off and I went crashing to the floor. I was in shock and so was my trainer. Still in shock, he managed to calmly pick me up and carry me to the locker room to gather myself. Somehow, I regained my composure. I emerged from the locker room with an embarrassed but determined attitude and committed to finish my workout.

As we marked the three and six months of evaluations, I noticed my progression. I was able to do basic routines and just needed guidance with new exercises or straight pull-ups. My life changed measurably with my overall health and emotional state—finally, my inward voice, that state of thoughts beyond your first level of reality and I was finally able to smile at myself.

My selves were in sync with one another. The feeling of accomplishment inwardly showed outwardly. My reflection wasn't a regurgitation to me. I saw both versions of me and chose a grin over a grimace. I woke up and began to love myself. It was a strange, but welcomed emotion.

I started to divide the chaos in my life and decompartmentalize it. One of the great Kingdom Commandments is to: Love God, Love Yourself, and Love Others. I always knew that God loved me, but doing self-care allowed me to love myself inwardly and love others outwardly.

Taking care of my body was a missing element to my success and living life. The commitment to work out at least four days a week shifted my thoughts. I was happily engrossed in eating healthier and limiting my sugar intake. I started to seek community associations with health-like individuals. The dramatic changes were affecting every area of my life. I started to visit local health shops. Gathering information on healthy options, workout tips, and development of relationships outside of my normal social circle. Shout out to the Herbal Life Family and establishments in G-town.

Suddenly the focus of my outward appearance was not only shaping me outwardly, but it was being developed from the inside out. My highest weight was around 240 pounds, and it started to come off steadily. My clothing size went from a 2xlarge to large over the next four years. My entire body was changing except for my stomach region. My total overall health was not perfect. As the weight came off, other issues surfaced. After years of neglecting my body, I fully understood that aches and pains were part of this transformation.

Commitment shined a light on other areas of my life where there was no such commitment. I realized that many in my life had a lack of commitment to me, but I was committed to them—the constant giving of myself to temporarily fill the void of loneliness. The awareness of my outward transformation began building me up on the inside. My tolerance level of people, places, and things was changing, and I isolated myself in other forms to block out any negativity concerning my goals.

I did not feel comfortable sharing my transformation experience. I did not allow anyone exclusively into my pain. My healing was too private to share. I just wanted to change without the judgment of others trying to convince me that things were already well.

My desires were now focused on a new phase of my life. As a result, I now struggled with allocating time to those things of the past. It was odd and painful but necessary. I just did not have time for those who were seeking to be in my company that did not have the similar goals of getting to a healthy place. I did not have time for people's foolish assumptions that there must be someone of interest as to why such a dramatic change in my life. Some of my associations had to change.

My body measurements began to change in ways that caused medical concerns with my prosthesis. The weight loss and muscle development caused the prosthesis' socket attachment to rub in sensitive areas. It started to cause gaps in my workouts, as those areas would heal. Three operations developed some setbacks during the following years, but I still had enough progress to keep pressing forward.

This one decision led me on a five-year journey of discovery. I was able to see measurable growth in my life. There were shifts in my personal and professional life during these years. Some decisions were questionable, but because of Romans 8:28, I knew that everything that was happening was working together for good because God loved me and my life had a divine call and deliberate purpose.

The phrase, "I'm living my best life," was my motto. My moments of isolation were not associated with loneliness. Instead, it was a pursuit of freedom and liberty that drew me into myself. I had begun to separate the light from the darkness in my life, worlds and affairs.

I was inspired me to relocate. I so embraced the Kingdom Principle of Divine Timing and Placement: Everything was unfolding exactly in the right time and place, there was no struggle to adjust my time to be in the spaces and places that led to inner growth. I craved holistic health.

Tuesday, October 30th, 2018, I received the final adjustments to the new prosthesis. I had finally gotten to a steady level of weight loss over the years. I had shed about 50 pounds over the last few years. This new prosthesis would give me a firm fitting and allow for next-level gait training and possibly the Broad Street Run, which is one of my goals. I worked out on a treadmill and participated in distance walking. I felt with some additional training and felt the Broad Street run would be possible in my near future, finally, after at least 20 years of not going to any form of therapy or gait training.

I agreed to see a therapist. Within the first five minutes of working with her, she noticed something that would change my life for the better. She had me do some distance walking and asked how long I had been walking with this profound limp, and I told her about 25 years. She called my prosthesis doctor and had him come over to the lab. She asked him to adjust the prosthesis length by 1.5 inches. This adjustment immediately corrected my stance, and my stance from years of profound limb loss was less noticeable. I stood with more stability. This correction made standing far more comfortable. My walking improved instantly. We had made various adjustments over the years and had no success in improving upon my limp. Six prostheses later and multiple consultations, I finally saw a substantial difference.

The weight loss, the muscle development, and a positive attitude all came into alignment, and my crooked movements were now coming into alignment. I know it was not complete elimination of the limp, but it sure felt like it. I conquered the fear and the shame of being an amputee. For the first time, I allowed the world to see me with it uncovered. It was freeing and liberating and I posted a photo on social media as a sign of conquest. This image was my declaration of independence.

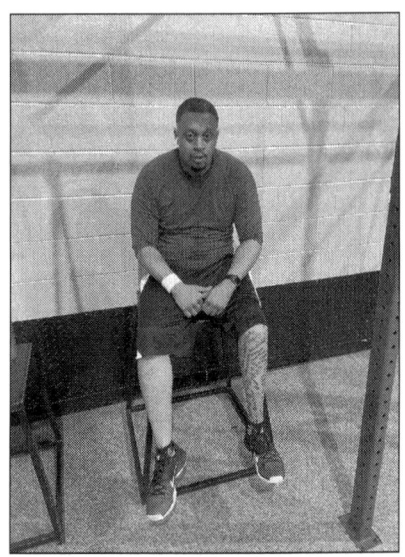

A combination of faith and determination is what got me to this point. Now, trust and perseverance will keep me pressing forward. I wore shorts during the summer of 2019 and started a campaign of awareness for other amputees. This campaign was to sign my prosthetic outer skin which helped to raise over three hundred dollars for amputees. I donated the money to the Thomas Jefferson Hospital.

The incorporation of Kingdom Living has become a part of my daily focus. Starting my day with meditation and prayer and allowing God to direct my daily living has truly been a blessing.

On the next pages are the principles and scriptures that have help me daily to correct a faulty limp, compensate for a phantom limb and create a full life.

KINGDOM PRINCIPLES OF DIVINE LIVING

The Kingdom Principle of Divine Nature. We believe the nature of God is love. We love God, ourselves, and everyone else. Who we are is Divine, created in the image and likeness of God (Matthew 22:34-40, John 10;30, Romans 8:38-39, Psalms 84:11).

The Kingdom Principle of Divine Purpose. We believe that the general Divine purpose for all life is to conform to the image of the Christ consciousness. Every being is also born with a Divine specific purpose, our why, to be discovered and fulfilled (John 10:10, Romans 8:28-29, I Corinthians 12:3-14, Galatians 5:22 -23, Ephesians 4:11-16, Romans 14:17, Luke 17: 20 -21).

The Kingdom Principle of Divine Order. There is a Divine Order in the universe, and everything that happens in this life is according to that Divine Order (Psalms 37:23, Galatians 6:6-10).

The Kingdom Principle of Divine Timing. There is a Divine Timing in the universe and that everything happens according to that Divine Timing (I Peter 5:6. Esther 4:14, Matthew 6:28-33)

The Kingdom Principle of Divine Placement. There is a Divine Placement in the universe. We are precisely where we are supposed to be spiritually, mentally, emotionally, physically, geographically, financially, educationally, vocationally, relationally, and socially (Philippians 4:11, I Timothy 6:6).

The Kingdom Principle of Divine Provision. God has already provided everything that we need naturally and spiritually. We believe that God is our Source of perfect health, wealth, and harmony in all relation-

ships (II Peter 1:3-4, Psalms 37:4, Philippians 4:19, Luke 6:38).

The Kingdom Principle of Divine Protection. *God divinely protects and encompasses us with a hedge of protection. Anything that gets through the hedge of protection to us was meant to be intended for God's glory and our good (Psalms 34:7, Job 1:10, II Timothy 1:7, Isaiah 54:17, Hebrews 13:6, Psalms 27:1-2).*

Here is a list of scriptures that helped me along the journey.

1. *Matthew 5:4 "Blessed are those who mourn, for they will be comforted."*
2. *John 14:27 "Peace I leave with you; my peace I give you. I do not give to you as the world gives. Do not let your hearts be troubled and do not be afraid."*
3. *Romans 8:35-39 "Who shall separate us from the love of Christ? Shall trouble or hardship or persecution or famine or nakedness or danger or sword? As it is written: "For your sake we face death all day long; we are considered as sheep to be slaughtered." No, in all these things we are more than conquerors through him who loved us. For I am convinced that neither death nor life, neither angels nor demons, neither the present nor the future, nor any powers, neither height nor depth, nor anything else in all creation, will be able to separate us from the love of God that is in Christ Jesus our Lord."*
4. *John 14:1-4 "Do not let your hearts be troubled. You believe in God; believe also in me. My Father's house has many rooms; if that were not so, would I have told you that I am going there to prepare a place for you? And if I go and prepare a place for you, I will come back and take you to be with me that you also may be where I am. You know the way to the place where I am going."*
5. *1 Corinthians 15:50-57 "I declare to you, brothers and sisters, that flesh and blood cannot inherit the kingdom of God, nor does the perishable inherit the imperishable. Listen, I tell you a mystery: We will not all sleep, but we will all be*

changed— in a flash, in the twinkling of an eye, at the last trumpet. For the trumpet will sound, the dead will be raised imperishable, and we will be changed. For the perishable must clothe itself with the imperishable, and the mortal with immortality. When the perishable has been clothed with the imperishable, and the mortal with immortality, then the saying that is written will come true: "Death has been swallowed up in victory." "Where, O death, is your victory? Where, O death, is your sting?" The sting of death is sin, and the power of sin is the law. But thanks be to God! He gives us the victory through our Lord Jesus Christ."

6. *Job 19:25-27* "I know that my redeemer lives, and that in the end he will stand on the earth. And after my skin has been destroyed, yet in my flesh I will see God; I will see him with my own eyes I, and not another. How my heart yearns within me!"

7. *Psalm 61:1-2* "Hear my cry, O God; listen to my prayer. From the ends of the earth, I call to you, I call as my heart grows faint; lead me to the rock that is higher than I." After I got the call that my baby sister had passed, I screamed in the middle of the Charlotte Douglas airport and cried like a baby for what seemed like hours. After I regained my composure, I recited the 23 Psalm for the entire plain ride to Philly.

8. *Psalm 23* (NKJV) "The Lord is my shepherd; I shall not want. He makes me to lie down in green pastures; He leads me beside the still waters. He restores my soul; He leads me in the paths of righteousness For His name's sake. Yea, though I walk through the valley of the shadow of death, I will fear no evil; For You are with me; Your rod and Your staff, they comfort me. You prepare a table before me in the presence of my enemies; You anoint my head with oil; My cup runs over. Surely goodness and mercy shall follow me All the days of my life; And I will dwell in the house of the Lord Forever."

9. *Lamentations 3:22-26, 31-33* "Because of the Lord's great love we are not consumed, for his compassions never fail. They are new every morning; great is your faithfulness.

10. *Psalm 121* "I lift up my eyes to the mountains—where does my help come from? My help comes from the Lord, the Maker of heaven and earth. He will not let your foot slip—he

who watches over you will not slumber; indeed, he who watches over Israel will neither slumber nor sleep. The Lord watches over you—the Lord is your shade at your right hand; the sun will not harm you by day, nor the moon by night. The Lord will keep you from all harm—he will watch over your life; the Lord will watch over your coming and going both now and forevermore."

11. Psalm 27:4-5 *"One thing I ask from the Lord, this only do I seek: that I may dwell in the house of the Lord all the days of my life, to gaze on the beauty of the Lord and to seek him in his temple. For in the day of trouble he will keep me safe in his dwelling; he will hide me in the shelter of his sacred tent and set me high upon a rock."*

12. Ecclesiastes 3:1-4 *For everything there is a season, and a time for every matter under heaven: a time to be born, and a time to die; a time to plant, and a time to pluck up what is planted; a time to kill, and a time to heal; a time to break down, and a time to build up; a time to weep, and a time to laugh; a time to mourn, and a time to dance*

13. Isaiah 41:10 *fear not, for I am with you; be not dismayed, for I am your God; I will strengthen you, I will help you, I will uphold you with my righteous right hand*

14. Corinthians 15:54-55 *When the perishable puts on the imperishable, and the mortal puts on immortality, then shall come to pass the saying that is written: "Death is swallowed up in victory." "O death, where is your victory? O death, where is your sting?"*

15. Revelation 21:4 *He will wipe away every tear from their eyes, and death shall be no more, neither shall there be mourning, nor crying, nor pain anymore, for the former things have passed away."*

16. Matthew 11:28 *"Come to me, all you who are weary and burdened, and I will give you rest."*

17. Lamentations 3:31-33 *"For no one is cast off by the Lord forever. Though he brings grief, he will show compassion, so great is his unfailing love. For he does not willingly bring affliction or grief to anyone."*

18. Romans 8:31-39 *"What, then, shall we say in response to these things? If God is for us, who can be against us? He who did not spare his own Son, but gave him up for us all—how will he not also, along with him, graciously give us all things? Who will bring any charge against those whom God*

has chosen? It is God who justifies. Who then is the one who condemns? No one. Christ Jesus who died—more than that, who was raised to life—is at the right hand of God and is also interceding for us. Who shall separate us from the love of Christ? Shall trouble or hardship or persecution or famine or nakedness or danger or sword? As it is written: "For your sake we face death all day long; we are considered as sheep to be slaughtered." No, in all these things we are more than conquerors through him who loved us. For I am convinced that neither death nor life, neither angels nor demons, neither the present nor the future, nor any powers, neither height nor depth, nor anything else in all creation, will be able to separate us from the love of God that is in Christ Jesus our Lord."

19. *2 Corinthians 5:17 Therefore if any man be in Christ, he is a new creature: old things are passed away; behold, all things are become new.*

IN THIS FINAL STAGE OF GRIEF, I LEARNED TO
"ACCEPT MY STANCE"
NOT ONLY DO I STAND. I STAND THEREFORE...
AND I AM POSTURED TO RUN!

CHAPTER SEVEN

THE KINGDOM MESSAGE
DR. DORAL R. PULLEY

According to Dr. Pulley's *Disciples of Christ Carrying their Cross,* any thought, word, behavior, substance, or relationship that does not promote abundant life and the Kingdom of God should be reduced, avoided, and/or eliminated through the seven spiritual disciplines of prayer, fasting, reading/studying the scriptures, praise and worship, stewardship, fellowship with the saints and witnessing to the lost (Pulley, 2008).

The word, discipline, comes from the word, disciple. A disciple is a disciplined follower of Christ. Before a disciple can move to leadership, the next stage of religious development, he or she must master the seven spiritual disciplines. The seven spiritual disciplines are prayer, fasting, reading and studying the scriptures, praise and worship, personal stewardship, fellowship with other disciples and witnessing to the lost. Although some spiritual disciplines come easier for some disciples and some spiritual disciplines are more challenging, a mature disciple must be actively engaged in all seven spiritual disciplines.

The seven spiritual disciplines is a positive approach to developing Christian character in the Non-denominational Christian Church. Instead of focusing on the things that a disciple should not do, this approach focuses on the things that the disciple should do. Using this approach, with very little effort, negative thoughts, words and behaviors decrease and some even cease. It is through the practice of the seven spiritual disciplines that the disciple becomes more and more like Christ and less and less like the world. Notice that all the seven spiritual disciplines are proactive. These are things that you must do as opposed to the things that you must stop doing. When I grew up in the church, the focus of the Christian life was to stop lying, fornicating, going to clubs, cursing, smoking, drinking, and all those sinful behaviors. The preachers kept preaching, "Stop this and stop that. Don't do this and don't do that." Very seldom did they tell us what we could do.

The Kingdom approach is a new approach to ministry that will accomplish the same goal of living a holy life, in a more effective, efficient, and empowering way. In Kingdom, people are not to focus on stopping anything. In fact, keep doing what you are doing until you outgrow it. However, we also tell them to keep coming to church, establish a prayer life, read the word daily, give God the glory, and doing all those other spiritual exercises. What we have noticed is that as they keep doing the positive things of the Spirit, that they outgrow the negative things of the flesh. They no longer desire or feel comfortable with the old behaviors.

The scripture, "and the yoke shall be destroyed because of the anointing (Isaiah 10:27)." It means that their necks had grown so fat that the yoke could no longer fit. As people grow spiritually, their necks grow so fat that their old lifestyle does not fit. What the church has done is forced hypocrisy. We tell people to stop behaviors because we are uncomfortable with their sin; God is not intimidated by people's sin. He knows their destiny and is bringing them along that path of wholeness.

When the church forces people to take off behaviors that still fit them, we are telling people to give up something that they still feel they may need and can't do without. We are telling them to pretend to appear righteous and holy, so that we can feel like they are saved. Nevertheless, when they are not around the saints, they go back and put on those same sinful behaviors because they still fit. However, if we allow people time and space to grow to maturity in spiritual things, they will take off sinful behaviors on their own and if they attempt to revert back, or put them back on, they themselves will discover that they don't fit anymore. In essence, because of the anointing, their neck outgrew the yoke of fornication, smoking, drinking, gossiping, etc. We must allow people the privilege of "growing in grace and in the knowledge of Jesus Christ (II Peter 3:18)."

According to Dr. Pulley's *Seven Stages of Creation*, God has created everything that exists in stages (Pulley, 2010). The Bible gives of seven stages of by which creation takes place: silence, thoughts, spoken word, action, evaluation, manifestation, and progression. We have the same power to create our lives and experiences by following these same stages.

Silence is more than just not speaking. Silence is holistic. Silence is quieting our bodies – every muscle, every organ, and every cell. Silence is quieting our souls – our minds, our emotions, our intellect, and our will. Silence is quieting our spirits – so that the Spirit of God can have God's way in our lives. When something good truly begins, we are silent. We are still. In this beginning, we are at a state of being, yielding and letting as opposed to doing, forcing, and making. It is only when we are truly silent and still that we "know that He is God (Psalms 46:10)."

Before God spoke anything into existence, God created it in mind first. Before God made anything, God **thought** about it. God created everything in mind first and then played it out day by day. Creation is an act of the mind. Silence is the ground. Thoughts are the seeds. We create our own lives through our thoughts. Whatever is going on in our lives right now, it all started with a thought. Whether we consider our current situation to be positive or negative, it all began with an idea (Proverbs 23:7). The beauty of the mind is that if we don't like what we have created, then we can change our minds and create something different. If we don't like the harvest, we can change the seed. It will take time to uproot what we have planted. Nevertheless, we can create a different life if we start thinking different thoughts, speaking different words and doing different deeds.

As we read the biblical account of the history of how things came to be in Genesis 1, there is a word that God says repeatedly in the process of creation, "Let." "Let" seems like a passive word because it means to allow things to be or to come into existence. It is not as forceful like its counterpart, "make." As God said, "Let there be..." the universe responded to His words and brought into being whatever God said. God is still speaking, and the universe is still responding to His words bringing into being whatever He says. "...My word that goes forth out of my mouth: it shall not return unto me void, but it shall accomplish that which I please, and it shall prosper in the thing whereto I sent it (Isaiah 55:11)."

God has given us a voice to speak God's **words** and the universe is responding to what we speak in the atmosphere. There is power and authority in our voice. Therefore, just as we learned last week to be good stewards over our minds and our thoughts, we must become good stewards over our mouths and our words. Our minds and our mouths work together to bring forth our harvest. Our thoughts and our words are in harmony to bring forth fruit.

Once God spoke the light into existence by saying, "Let there be light," God separated the light from the darkness which was an **action**. He called the darkness night and the light he called day. Later, God separated the light to determine time: days, years, and seasons. Then God further separated the lights of the day into two lights: the sun and the moon. The daytime, the nighttime, the sun, the moon, the stars, days, seasons, and years were all created from one thing, light. God pulled all these things from the light. Once God separated light into these various dimensions, God gave each aspect of light a name and a specific purpose.

We must follow God's example and realize that the things that we create are pregnant with several other possibilities. We must take the time to examine our creations and see all the potential within each creation. We must separate each aspect of our creation and give it its own name and purpose. All of us are God's creation. Within each of us are several gifts, talents and abilities. Let's open up our hearts and minds to see the vast potential in everything that is created. As co-creators with God, after we speak things into existence, the next stage of bringing things into being is activity. This stage requires a greater level of sensitivity to the Holy Spirit. Only through listening and being led by the Spirit will we know exactly what type of activity is needed to bring about our manifestation. Sometimes the activity is totally in the Spirit and all we must go with the flow. Other times the activity is something that we must do in conjunction with the Spirit (James 2:26).

Everything that God created in His mind in the beginning, manifested, it happened. And God said, "Let there be light and there was light (Genesis 1:5)." As we read Genesis 1, at the end of just about every day of creation are the words, "and it was so (Genesis 1:7, 9, 11, 15, 24 and 30)." Whether God spoke it into existence like the light or He did some type of action to bring it forth like human beings, everything that God created **manifested**; it came into being.

In the Spirit everything is already done. God has already given us "all things that pertain unto life and godliness through the knowledge of Him who has called us to glory and virtue (II Peter 1:3)." However, all the things that God has given us are in the spiritual realm. All the blessings of God are invisible. All our prayers are already answered in the heavenly places. Just because it exists, does not mean that it has **manifested.**

The word, manifestation, means a visible change or a difference that can be experienced by at least one of the five senses (seeing, hearing, touching, tasting, and smelling). When the gifts that God has given us are moved from the spiritual realm to the natural realm, we call it manifestation. When the invisible blessings of God become visible, we call it manifestation. When our answered prayers are no longer in the heavenly places but are tangible on the earth, we call it **manifestation.**

After the light manifested, God **evaluated** the light by seeing it and saying that "it was good." God follows this same pattern with the water, the sky, the land, the animals, and the trees. At the close of each of the first five days of creation, God evaluates His creation and calls it good before He moves to the next day and the next creation. When God calls one of the creations good, He is saying that it is fulfilling the purpose for which He created it. When God calls His creation good, He is saying that the manifestation is adequately reflecting the original vision that He had in His mind about it. At the end of the sixth day, after God finished making man and woman, God calls His creation something different. He calls the man and the woman very good because they met different criteria. Human beings are more than just good because they are the only creation that was actually made in His image and after His likeness. Human beings are different from all other creations because we have higher level thinking skills and the ability to make decisions. We must follow God's example and have criteria for evaluating our creations to determine whether they are good or very good.

After God evaluated His creation and determined that it was good or very good, God **progressed** to the next dimension. God's progression cannot be put into a box and does not always follow the exact same pattern. Depending on what God is creating, His progression can mean so many different things. Sometimes God's progression is enhancing something that He has already made. Other times, God's progression means moving on to create something entirely new and different. God's progression can also be destroying an old creation and recreating it into something new. Another aspect of God's progression is getting to a place where He could rest from His labor. Regardless of the form that **progression** takes, God is always progressive. God is never stuck. God is never stagnant. God is never static. God is never without a plan. God is always moving on and moving forward to the next...

As we walk in the Spirit and go with the flow of life, we must always be **progressive**. We cannot afford to get stuck in the feelings of guilt, shame and/or condemnation. We must learn from our mistakes and not waddle in them so that we can progress to the next step of our journey. We cannot afford to be stagnant in the process of our holistic growth and development. Anything that is alive is always growing and changing. We cannot afford to be static in the old or keep laying the same foundation over and over again. At some point, we must progress. At some point, we must build the house. We cannot afford to be without a plan. As we move forward, God keeps unfolding what the next step is and His word becomes "a lamp unto our feet and light unto our path (Psalms 119:105)." As we walk in the ordered steps (Psalms 37:23), God gives us a plan and direction for our future.

The Difference between the World, the Church, and the Kingdom

As described in Dr. Pulley's *Stepping into the Next Dimension*, the word, kingdom, is a combination of two words, king and domain (Pulley, 2013). The kingdom is the king's domain. It is where the king rules, reigns and has dominion. **The Kingdom of God is where God rules and reigns**. It is not a physical place or location, but it is a system, a form government, a lifestyle and a way of being. The Kingdom of God is wherever God's perfect will is being done. Jesus taught His disciples to pray, "Thy Kingdom come, thy will be done in earth as it is in heaven (Matthew 6:10)." **When God's will in heaven (Kingdom of Heaven) is being done on the earth (in our lives), it is a manifestation of the Kingdom of God.** Jesus came to the earth as our Way shower to reveal the Father to us and show us what heaven was like so that we realize who we are as children of God, living according to Kingdom principles (Matthew 11:27).

The Kingdom of God is a way of being, seeing, thinking, speaking and behaving in which God is the center.
As Kingdom citizens, we have the mind of Christ (I Corinthians 2:16). Unlike the people of the Old Testament, whose ways were not God's ways and whose thoughts were not God's thoughts, because of Jesus' example, the written Word and the indwelling of the Spirit of God, we can think God's thoughts and operate according to His ways (Isaiah 55:8 -9). Because we are one with God, His thoughts become our thoughts and our ways become His ways (John 10:30, I Corinthians 6:17). As a husband and wife through a process become one flesh, through our relationship with God we manifest our oneness with Him.

As citizens of the Kingdom, we can also speak God's words and frame "our world" according to our words just as God created the world by His words (Hebrews 11:3). Death and life are in the power of our own tongues and we determine what takes place in our lives by the words that we speak (Proverbs 18:21). As kings and priests, God is also the center of our behaviors and our actions are reflections of Kingdom principles (Revelation 1:6). As kings of the Kingdom, we operate according to God's ways and live according to the leading of the Holy Spirit (Romans 8:14). Living the Kingdom life means that our lives are centered on God, not around any other person, place or thing. As Kingdom people, when we lose focus or get distracted, we center ourselves in His presence through the spiritual disciplines of prayer/meditation, fasting, praise and worship, reading and studying the Word, etc. (Psalms 16:1).

The Kingdom of God is righteousness, peace and joy in the Holy Ghost (Romans 14:17).
The Kingdom of God is an internal knowing that we are in right relationship with God and that nothing can separate us from the love of God (Romans 8:35-38). The Kingdom of God is loving ourselves and being in right relationship with ourselves. We manifest the Kingdom of God and demonstrate our

role as Kingdom Directors through our diet, intimacy (revealing our true selves to others), rest (getting enough sleep to function at our optimum), eating properly, check-ups with doctors and dentists, treating ourselves, outward appearance (hygiene and appearance) and relaxing (having fun), that illustrates the manifestation of the Kingdom of God in our lives. The Kingdom of God is being in right relationship with others by loving and accepting all people and treating them the way that we want to be treated. The Kingdom of God is an internal peace that regardless to what is going on externally that we have peace within that can't be disrupted by chaos or disturbed by confusion. The Kingdom of God is an internal joy that regardless of sorrow or daily happenings that we are strengthened by an unspeakable joy (I Peter 1:8). The Kingdom of God is inside of us because the Holy Ghost is inside of us and inside of the Holy Ghost is everything that we need and desire (II Pet 1:3-5).

Just as it is important to understand what the Kingdom of God is, it is just as essential to understand what the Kingdom of God is not. Sometimes to have a full picture of what something is, we have to look closely at what it is not. Many people confuse the Kingdom of God with the church, the world, heaven and earth. Nevertheless, the Kingdom of God is not the church. The Kingdom of God is not the world. The Kingdom of God is not heaven. The Kingdom of God is not the earth. The Kingdom of God is not a physical place and has no address. The Kingdom of God is within us (Luke 17:20-21).

The Kingdom of God is not the Church, locally or globally.

The local assembly is a gathering of members of the Body of Christ and people of the world for the purpose of corporate worship and praise (Matthew 18:18-20). The Body of Christ worldwide is the sum total of all baptized believers (I Corinthians 12:13). The Kingdom of God is so much bigger than people whether it is a local gathering or a global sum. The Kingdom of God also includes the angels in heaven and wherever God's perfect will is done. Nevertheless, the church is the entrance way to the Kingdom because the keys to the Kingdom were given to the Church (II Peter 1:11, Matthew 16:13-

20). People go from the world into the church and then into the Kingdom. The church is the mid-point between the world and the Kingdom.

The Kingdom of God is not the world.

The world is the total opposite of the Kingdom of God. The world is not the flowers, birds, the seas, and the land. The world is a system, a form of government, a way of being, seeing, thinking, speaking, and behaving that excludes God. The center of the world is immediate gratification and self-pleasures even to the detriment of God, self and others (I John 2:15-17). The world opposes God's will, purpose, and plan. It is impossible to be friends with God and friends with the world (James 4:4). Jesus declared, "My kingdom is not of this world. (John 18:36)" Therefore, He and His disciples did not respond to issues the way the world did. Jesus, our Way shower, lived His life not according to the traditions of world or the rituals of Judaism but by Kingdom principles.

The Kingdom of God is not the earth.

God created the heavens, the earth and all that is in them (Genesis 1:1). The earth belongs to Him, but he gave human beings dominion over the earth (Psalms 24:1-3, Genesis 1:26). Because God has given humanity the gifts of free will and choice, we can choose to do God's will or not. The earth has been destroyed by water and the earth will be destroyed again by fire due to the wickedness of man's heart and our opposition to God's will (Genesis 9:11, II Peter 3:10-13). After the destruction of the earth, God will establish a new earth where His purposes will be accomplished without sin, sickness, pain, sorrow, poverty or death (Revelation 21:1-2). In the new earth, human beings will be given crowns (positions of authority) to rule, reign and have dominion based on their works on the old earth. The Alpha is the Omega. Just as things were with Adam and Eve in the Garden of Eden, we will return to a place of complete oneness with God in a state of euphoria and bliss.

The Kingdom of God is not heaven.

Heaven is known as the place where God dwells (Psalms 11:4). Just as earth was created in perfection so was heaven. However, heaven was contaminated by Lucifer's ego and sin (Isaiah 14:12-15, Job 1:6). Therefore, he and all the angels who followed him were disbanded from heaven. After his death, burial and resurrection, Jesus purified heaven with his blood and prepared a place for us to have access to heavenly places (John 14:1-6, 20:17, Hebrews 9:23-24). Nevertheless, the old heaven will be destroyed, and we will have a new heaven just as we will have a new earth that is committed to the glory and worship of God (Revelation 21:1). The kingdoms of this world are become the kingdoms of our Lord, and of his Christ; and he shall reign for ever and ever (Revelation 11:15).

The Kingdom of God is not meat or drink (Romans 14:17).

The Kingdom of God is not anything that we can experience with our physical senses. We can't see the Kingdom of God with our natural eyes, it is invisible. We can't hear the Kingdom of God with our natural ears. We can't touch the Kingdom of God with our natural hands. We can't taste or experience the Kingdom of God with our natural mouths or lips. We cannot smell the Kingdom of God with our noses. The Kingdom of God is those spiritual qualities of love, righteousness, joy and peace that can only be experienced internally and in the spiritual realm. As Paul, an apostle of Jesus Christ, tried to convey to the saints in Romans 14, the Kingdom of God is not about what day you worship on or what you eat or what you wear or what type of music you listen to or who you are attracted to or how you baptize. These are all church isms and schism that have absolutely nothing to do with the Kingdom of God. Each person must be fully persuaded in his or her own mind and answer to God as it relates to these matters (Romans 14:5). All these issues are externals and temporary. The Kingdom of God is internal and everlasting.

DON'T TAKE MY WORD FOR IT
"IN THEIR OWN WORDS..."

Mother Arlene Williams

Early in the morning of January 22, 1993, I received a phone call stating my son, Teto had been shot. His father jumped out of the bed to rush to University of Pennsylvania Hospital. We did not know what to expect, but he was alive. Thank God! I prayed that he would be alive when we arrived. I did not know the circumstances but was told he was shot in the leg, and it looked bad. I was out of my mind. I asked God to save my son and He did just that. He lost his leg but he was still alive. I thank God for his life. It was not an easy road to recovery, but he made it; through prayer and many tears. I know that prayer works. I know prayer works because he did it for me and my family and countless others who stood on the wall for us. Today my son is a Bishop in the Lord's Church preaching and teaching. What does that say of the Lord my God? He is an awesome God! He brought my son through it all.

Bishop-elect Yolanda Johnson-Jenkins

Out of the cascading layers of darkness shined down a light to guide our future away from our fears. Picture a forest of trees side by side towering over you. You are not able to find your shadow. You search desperately for reassurance that each step you take diminishes the doubt in your mind about your survival. The one true hope that never leaves you is the Sun's streaming light through the crowded canopies of the trees. The light seems faint at times as you move cautiously swift through the forest, but it never fails; it is always there and seeks out to rescue you into your clear path of openness. The light is God; the light is also Bishop Teto T. Saunders through his journey of loss and reclamation. Twenty- seven years ago a young man by the name of Teto T. Saunders; adoringly known as Teet by his family and me; underwent a tumultuous event.

Due to the aftermath of city violence and encountering a desperate soul on 52nd & Addison Street; a sawed off shot gun's pellets penetrated his flesh relentlessly and without remorse. The weapon made no apology for its actions.

I found out the next day as I sat in my 12th grade class. Worry clouded my judgement. Fear overtook my sight and doubt reminded me that death could be near. Rushing to the hospital afterschool unaware if my presence would even be noticed, accepted, or needed; I simply went.

In my going to visit Teto week upon week and month upon month, he would eventually pick himself up from that darkened forest and take one step at a time into his future. Having undergone many surgeries, doctor visits, physical therapy and all that is assigned to traumatic experiences he moved swiftly but with caution towards his reassurance. He moved just like the sunlight in the forest; only shining light on the dark places that needed illumination so that he could find his way to his path.

When I relive in my mind the dynamic impact Teto T. Saunders forces you to have with your own destiny I realize that the power of belief lies so deep within himself. The presence of God then and the presence of God now has opened his forest of life. In that forest is his road to recovery. In that forest is his attachment to help others. In that forest is his tears, fears, agony, growth, and pain. In that forest is the limb that was removed and the life he gained. In that forest is his heart for people of all origins. In that forest Teto. T. Saunders became a prism; God's light passing through and onward into his destiny yet ever so powerful to continue shine light for others as well.

Elder Evelyn Edwards
Like the energizer bunny going, going, and keeps going! I first met Teto in March 2014 while at the cafeteria at the Abramson Research Center cafeteria at The Children's Hospital of Philadelphia in line getting a cup of coffee. Teto was the per-

son at the register serving the customers such as I. I over-heard his conversation about him opening a church. I said to myself "hmmm how can he be a pastor when sometimes I come down here and he has a facial expression of being mad". Well, that was my judgement, judging the man from the out-side. I was totally wrong. The look he had was his business manager look.

He inspired me so from that conversation that I spoke to him about me coming to visit his church because I wanted to get reconnected to God as I was born and raised as a Catholic and did not learn much. Little did I know, I ended up joining his church on the ribbon cutting service of New Birth FTC, 2247 South 71st Street, Philadelphia PA at the 3:00pm hour. His spiritual father the late Bishop Robert M. Taylor was the guest speaker. I joined because I felt something over my body, not because I was a customer at the job. I noticed he had a limp and not knowing he had a prosthesis, but it did not distract me. If anything, I was amazed that this man can work on his feet all day with many late nights of catering, what was wrong with me with 2 good legs, always complaining.

I recently celebrated my 16th church anniversary at New Birth FTC, where Teto is the Bishop and Presiding Bishop of New Birth Fellowship Alliance. Throughout these 16 years, I have seen Bishop Saunders transform from that to this. With the unforeseen incident he experienced with getting shot and was pronounced clinically dead 3 times, all I can share is that this is a man of integrity, a man that does not allow NOTHING to stop him. This man taught and groomed me and many others how to pray, how to make a few dollars from a shiny or dirty penny.

This man was holding up traffic in Chester selling waters with his prosthetic leg. This man got in the pool with the youth dur-ing one of our convocations. This man has much wisdom and knowledge. This man was shy and did not talk much about his experience and now he has grown so much in his spiritual jour-ney that has caused him to become a stronger person, a man in the natural that is allowing him to be open about his experience and sharing his story with others who have a prosthesis. He sits as a peer with patients who recently had or will have a limb loss. This is a man of God!

Throughout these 16 years, I learned that Bishop Saunders has a heart of gold, a heart of helping others such as myself who experienced 4 transitions of family members: father, 1st husband, brother, sister, the 7 surgeries I had in 2017 and even through my current divorce. Bishop Saunders has been by myside through ALL my challenges speaking life into me saying "I Believe God", you are going to make it.

Bishop is a huge inspiration to many people, especially the Limb Loss patients. They look up to him because he keeps on going, going, and going as the "energizer man" from being a family working man, to a man who goes to the gym frequently. This man is a blessing to us all.
May God continue to order his footsteps as well as helping all people, not only those who suffer mentally from losing a limb as he assists them throughout the process.

Donna Drain
When I first met Bishop Teto T. Saunders, I did not know he had a prosthesis. I thought it was just a limp. Within the first few months of me attending his church at New Birth FTC, he began talking about it. I never looked at it as a disability, but his ability to allow the world to see that nothing can hold him back from achieving his accomplishments in life.

I have seen him transform from a shy person and become open about his prosthesis to showing it to the world.

He gives me inspiration that all things are possible. To never let anything stop me from helping people even though they hurt me. I will continue to help looking pass what was meant to stop me he has inspired to push me to continue doing what I do with helping others.

I look at Bishop Saunders and think that nothing can stop him.

Deacon George L. Boston, Jr.

Hearts and mind were clear, and I spoke up saying "no pastor I would like to say something if you don't mind". As I stated how humble Pastor Saunders is, he said George come on up. I took him up on his offer and I made my request known and from that day to this one, I have been right there with Bishop Teto T. Saunders. I have learned so much since I have been at New Birth FTC. I have been blessed to wear a few hats under his awesome tutelage: pastors' aide, licensed minister, ordained deacon. I totally trust Bishop Saunders with my life.

He is truly a hard-working prayer warrior and an awesome friend and most of all a man of God with a big heart who gives of his own personal time to share his talents, resources, and prayers. He knows me by my name. We sit down and talk. He has not only been good to me, but to my family in many big ways.

I am forever grateful to God for this man of God.

Pastor Stacey Caison

When I think of Teto the very first word that comes to mind is resilient, which is defined in the Merriam-Webster dictionary as, " tending to recover from or adjust easily to misfortune or change. Webster should add a picture of Teto next to the definition.

I remember the evening I received the phone call that he had gotten shot and was rushed to the hospital not knowing if he was going to make it or not. After numerous hospitals stays, multiple surgeries it seemed like a lifetime since I had seen him. Not knowing for myself his mental state just rumors from the few that he would allow to see him. I stayed my distance because I have always known him to be this strong and cocky guy.

One summer afternoon the young people from Fellowship Tabernacle Church were having a get together at Bishop Taylor's house. A bunch of us were in the swimming pool and Teto was on the trampoline doing what looked like martial arts. This was the first time I seem him without his prosthesis/prosthetic on. After a few slicks moves he dived into the swimming pool. It was at that moment I knew he was that strong cocky dude that I had grown to know and love. But now he has this "I can rule the world" attitude that seems bigger than life.

Through tragedy emerged this man of faith and purpose. He would speak about faith all the time and how he could overcome anything. Through his ministry I seen him minister to all kinds of people, especially to those that suffer from amputation for whatever reason. He is so open to share his story and experiences. Mind you he is a very private person, so I knew it had to be God for him to open and tell his story on so many different platforms.

Witnessing the transformation of this young man into this mighty man of God that speaks with so much authority was amazing. I see him pray and snap his fingers and the living God would move on command. I cannot count the numerous times he went into hospital rooms and delivered, he would pray, and people would be delivered and set free.

I remember when he spoke life over me. I was at a chemotherapy treatment feeling drained emotionally and mentally tired. Unknowing to me my Aunt Temple had asked him to come to Fox Chase to sit with me. His very presence changed the atmosphere. Not only did he pray over me, but he also prayed for my family, the other patients, and the staff. It was nothing less than a miracle. Myself along with the patient sitting next to me started laughing and talking about all the things we were going to do once our treatments where complete. I remember one of the nursing staff asking who was that? I said, my brother Pastor Saunders. She was amazed that such a young man spoke with so much authority when he prayed.

Bishop Teto Saunders has been an example of strength and a rock for me personally. During every major event that has taken place throughout my entire adult life, such as the loss of my mother, my sister and our spiritual father Apostle Robert Taylor, Sr. he has been there despite the challenges he was dealing with in his life.

Clarence A. Jones

I have known Teto Saunders for the better part of 35 years. Our friendship transcended to a brotherhood shortly thereafter. Teto was there for me like no other person. He watched, counseled, and supported me through all the trials and tribulations that young black men are frequently faced with when trying to figure out who they are, and how they will make their mark on the world. He was a role model for me. He was candid and to the point. I watched him graduate high school, graduate college, and always supported his family. Back then before the incident, at that time in my life, I relied heavily on his support. For me, he provided emotional support and sometimes financial support as I was attempting to follow in his footsteps and find success as a college student.

Teto has always possessed those leadership qualities. Along with myself, I personally saw him help and support a few other young men that were growing up in similar circumstances. From what I remember, these young men were co-workers and later, subordinates that he saw potential in and made the personal investment in helping to guide these young men in the right direction and not allow them to become a statistic.

Teto would go to college during the week, then commute back home on the weekends and work. At the time of his incident, I was away at college approximately 90 minutes away. When I first heard about him being shot, there was a huge sense of disbelief. I was clearly in denial that anything bad would happen to my brother. I did not know what to do. I was frozen. Myself and my former college roommate, who is also a friend of

Teto's, traveled from Dover, Delaware to Philadelphia shortly thereafter, to visit him in the hospital. Prior to departure, we were notified that Teto's leg would be amputated. That news was devastating. Immediately, I began to reflect on all the years of my friendship and how this incident will affect Teto moving forward. I thought about how he used his legs in the past, whether that was from running cross-country to being the main attraction at a party as far as dancing to practicing wrestling moves through his impersonation of stars such as Ric Flair. This incident was a life changer.

When I first arrived at the hospital, I remember having conversations with his family in the lobby. They provided some additional details about the incident. At the time, Teto was heavily sedated and was in and out of consciousness. I cannot remember the exact details of the first conversation that I had with him at the hospital, but I knew that I was an emotional wreck. Teto had helped me out of multiple bad situations in the past and now I did not know what to say or how to reciprocate. Teto was always there for me, and I am failing him. I felt that other people that did not have as close of a bond as I had with him were doing more to help him to make it through his ordeal. I was disgusted with myself because I stood there dumbfounded. I had so many mixed emotions from hate, shock, apathy, sadness, remorse, and many others. The problem was that I could not clearly articulate these. I felt helpless because I could not help my brother.

As I reflect on what occurred almost 30 years ago, I understand that I was quite immature and not very emotionally intelligent at that time. In my opinion, this incident placed a fracture on my relationship with Teto. We had a few discussions after, and he was able to share with me some of his thoughts. His disappointment with some things opened my eyes to areas that I was previously oblivious to. Teto is a shining example of resilience and perseverance. Once I matured and the lightbulb turned on, I became a better man because of him. I recently completed a 25 ½ - year career in the U.S. Army. I believe that my leadership style and approach was shaped to some degree, because of this incident and all the life lessons that it taught me. Today, I take a ton of pride in being emotionally, socially, and culturally aware. Also, it is of the utmost importance to be a good citizen that strives to serve as a model for integrity and honor. I give credit for that to Teto. I am so proud of the fact that he did not allow this incident to stop his progress and his mission to serve. Also, I am glad that he has strengthened his relationship with God and is serving as a minister spreading the gospel. Bishop Tcto Saunders is and always will be, my hero.

A REVIEW OF THE BOOK

Cast Down but not Destroyed is not just a book about overcoming challenges and obstacles but it is a self-help guide of discovery; a Manual depicting the reality in and between each stage of grief; a Tale of Triumph and finally, a Chronicle mapping the road to Victory.

In this magnificently written body of work, Bishop Saunders invites us into his most private spaces, courageously and transparently, as he is processed, pressed, and ultimately presented back to us and the world as a Victor- a Man, made whole. This is a must-read for anyone and everyone who may wonder if God can so that He can prove through this testimony of Triumph, that God did.

-Adriann Just The Pen Bautista
Author of Sanctuary of Snow and Sister Strength

A REVIEW OF THE BOOK

The eye and the mind will often shield us from the vulnerability of the ones we love. Have you ever wondered what was behind the cloth? What would you see In a man when undressed from the expectations, influences, support, ego, and even the ignorance of others? Well; Bishop Teto T. Saunders embraces the very personal and private places in the soul of his character.

We many times equate mourning to the loss of life excluding other manifestations of removing, losing and being without. He sojourns on a path of emotional, physical, intellectual, and spiritual truths that are awaken when he is forced into a place of danger, loss, and bittersweet birthing.

Something was taken from him, and he did not have the opportunity to share whether he agreed with it. Allow the words on the page to take you places that many of us would be uneasy to share. It is a place where real- lives. It is a place where pain cries blood. It is a place where blood cries for mercy. It is a place where mercy will carry you as you heal.

Don't be afraid to look at the man, with the man, and undoubtedly see yourself in a man. A man who unfolds his truth and healing.

Bishop-elect Yolanda Johnson-Jenkins
Promising Beauty

ABOUT THE BOOK AND THE AUTHOR
THE TRAUMA & TESTIMONY | THE TROPHY & TRUIMPH

"Cast Down but not Destroyed" reveals the twenty-five-year journey of a twenty-two-year-old man who loss his left leg above the knee to senseless gun violence on the streets of Philadelphia. It will detail my experiences within the five stages of grief: denial, anger, bargaining, depression, and acceptance. It will also feature testimonials of those who witness the journey firsthand.

ABOUT THE AUTHOR

Teto Thomas Saunders has over 25 + years of life experience as an above the knee amputee. He is the Set-Gift and Pastor of New Birth Fellowship Tabernacle Church and Presiding Bishop of the New Birth Fellowship Alliance, with global outreach ministries. He is a graduate of Widener University with a Bachelor of Science in Hospitality Management, and currently in pursuit of his Master and Doctorate in Global Leadership. He is the proud father of three children, Leonard, Cornelius, and William and he is also a grandfather.